Magical Unicorn
Spot the Difference

Sam Loman

ARCTURUS

ARCTURUS

This edition published in 2018 by Arcturus Publishing Limited
26/27 Bickels Yard, 151–153 Bermondsey Street,
London SE1 3HA, UK

Illustrated by Sam Loman
Written by Anna Brett
Edited by Susannah Bailey
Designed by Square and Circus

ISBN: 978-1-78888-153-1
CH006435NT
Supplier 29, Date 0818, Print run 7743

Printed in China

Best Friends Forever

These two unicorns are best friends! They try to always look the same, but can you find six differences between them?

Rainbow Magic

Unicorns can change their hair to match the stripes in a rainbow!
Spot ten differences between these two eye-catching scenes.

Cupcake Count

The unicorns are setting the table for cake, but one of their yummy treats looks a bit different. Can you work out which one?

Beautiful Butterflies

These butterflies have just hatched, and are spreading their wings for the first time. Can you spot six differences between the two scenes?

KITTEN KISSES

Willow has come to visit her cat friend, Cloudy, and her new kittens!

They are so much fun, climbing over everything in sight.
Can you see ten differences between these two images?

Reindeer Replacements

Santa's reindeer are sick! Luckily he's called on his unicorn friends to help pull the magic sleigh tonight.

Can you spot ten differences between the two scenes, as Santa delivers his gifts?

Little Ones

All the mothers have brought their babies along to the meadow to play together.
Can you see six differences between the two pictures?

Fancy Dress

These unicorns are all dressing up as fairies for the Midsummer party!
Can you spot which one has not got her costume quite right?

SPARKLING SEA

The unicorns are having a boat party!

Can you find ten things that have changed in the second picture?

Dream Wings

Unicorns love to dream that they can fly
high in the sky, in and out of the clouds.

Can you spot ten differences between
these two dreams?

Quickstep

Twinkletoes is trying to copy Stardust's dance moves, but she's got three of the steps wrong. Can you identify which three she needs to work on?

Winter Wonderland

It's snowing! Time to build some snow-unicorns, but watch out for the snowball fight! Can you see six differences in the second scene?

Falling Leaves

Moondust is dancing in the leaves at dusk. Can you spot ten differences between these wonderful woods?

Splish Splash

The unicorns are playing with the mermaids in the rock pool today.
Find ten differences between the two watery scenes.

BEACH BAG

It's time to hit the beach! Which unicorn's bag
is looking slightly different from the rest?

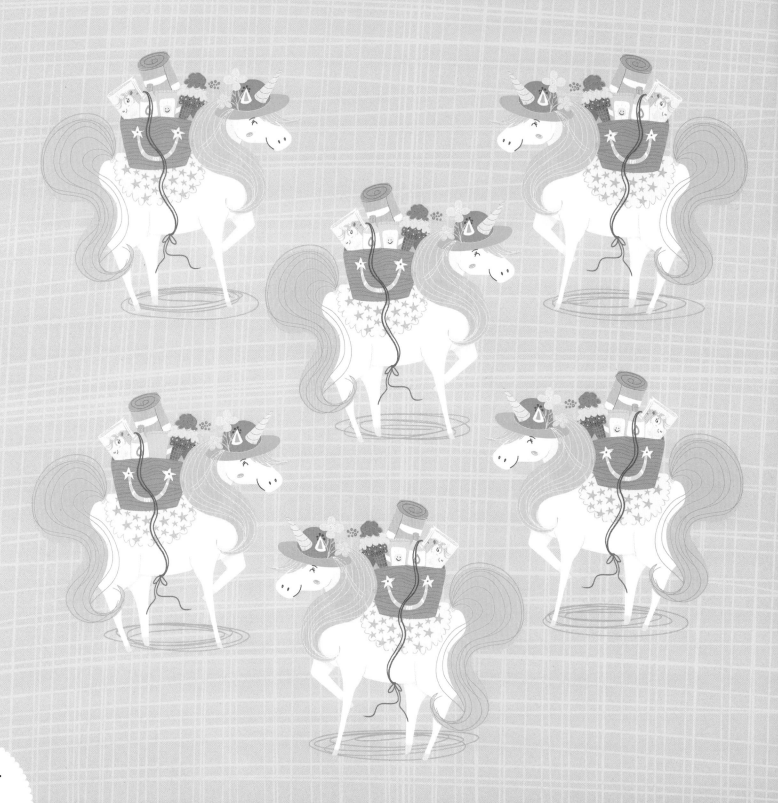

Love Is in the Air

Cupid is spreading love today, and everyone is thinking of their loved ones!
Can you spot six differences between the two scenes?

Brothers and Sisters

These puppy pets are all from the same litter!
Can you spot the ten differences between the two scenes?

Sleepover Snuggles

These three unicorns are having a sleepover tonight.

They look so comfy with their soft blankets, puffy cushions, and sweet treats.
Study the pictures and see if you can find all ten differences.

TIME TO SHINE

Glitter has just completed a perfect round at the competition! Sunray's round was not so successful. Can you see the three mistakes she made?

Prize Giving

It's time for the Rainbow Awards! There are six differences between the two ceremonies—can you spot them all?

Salon Style

It's busy in the Picture Perfect salon today, as Snowflake wants her manes and tail decorated.

Study the two scenes, then see if you can
spot all ten differences.

Fairy Ring

It's Midsummer's Eve, and the fairies are starting their party!

Can you find the ten differences
between the two gatherings?

CLOUD SPOTTING

These unicorns are looking up at the clouds in the sky. When the wind blows, the shapes change. See if you can find six changes in the second picture.

Flower Arranging

These two bouquets of flowers are being delivered to the palace, but they should match. Can you see the four flowers that are arranged differently?

Princess Palace

These unicorns can't wait to visit the pink palace today.
Can you spot ten differences between these royal scenes?

Whiz, Pop, Bang!

The unicorns are enjoying watching fireworks in the sky.

The magical display changes quickly, though. Can you spot the ten differences in the second image?

LUCKY CAKES

These cupcakes have been decorated with lucky unicorn shoes.
Three of the decorations are upside down—can you spot them?

Flower Crown

Sunshine has made a flower crown for Blossom.
See if you can find six things that have changed in the second image.

43

Round and Round

Unicorns love riding on rollercoasters ... as long as the loop-the-loop
doesn't make them too dizzy!

Can you spot ten differences between
these two speedy rides?

Birthday Party

It's Starshine's birthday, and her unicorn friends have arranged
a surprise party for her!

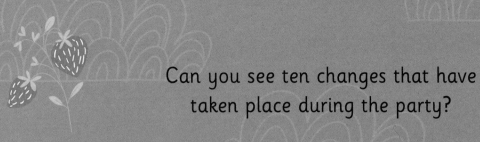

Can you see ten changes that have
taken place during the party?

47

OPEN WATER

These mermaids are going on a trip away from their home on the reef. Can you spot six differences between the swimming scenes?

Puppy Pairs

This unicorn is babysitting seven cute puppies. Three pairs are twins—can you match them up? Who doesn't have a twin?

Shopping Trip

It's time to hit the shops with your best unicorn friends!

Can you find ten differences between these two
super-fun shopping scenes?

End of the Rainbow

These unicorns have found the magical end of the rainbow!

It's beautiful, but can you spot ten things that
have changed in the second image?

Fairy Dust

The Fairy Godmother is sprinkling magic on Bluebell to make her even more pretty for a special party. Can you work out what change took place after each wave of the wand?

Royal Jewels

The princess is showing her unicorn friend all her beautiful jewels.
Can you find six differences between the two boxes?

Ice Skating

Unicorns love to skate—slipping and sliding is so much fun!

Not everyone is always steady on their hooves. Can you spot ten differences in the second image?

Ballet School

Point those hooves, and twirl that tail! Ballet class is in full swing.

Spot ten differences between the two images.

KITTEN TANGLE

These cute kitties are playing with their unicorn friend.
Can you find six differences between the two scenes?

Perfect Patterns

These unicorns have had their hooves and bodies painted! They all have matching designs, except for one. Who looks different?

Christmas Carols

Fa la la, it's time for the annual carol concert! There are ten differences between these two festive scenes—can you see them?

Sweet Dreams

What do unicorns dream about at night? Study the picture to find out, but also see if you can find ten differences!

BUTTERFLIES AND BEES

It's springtime, and the bees and butterflies are playing in the beautiful blooms.
Every creature has a twin, apart from one. Can you find it?

Yummy Ice Creams

It's hot today! All the unicorns are enjoying ice creams to help them to cool down. What are the six differences between the two scenes?

Fairground Fun

Roll up, roll up. There's so much to do at the fair!

Can you spy ten changes between the two scenes?

Coral Reef

Take a deep breath, and dive underwater to see all the
amazing marine life on the reef.

What ten things change as the
unicorns swim along?

SKI SLOPE

Slip and slide down the slope on skis. Can you spot the six differences in this snowy scene?

Uni-yoga

Unicorns love a good stretch! One of these members of the yoga class hasn't quite got the pose right—can you work out which one?

Gingerbread House

Deep in the forest, there's a secret gingerbread house.

It looks as if unicorns may have sampled some of the sweet decorations in the second picture! Can you spot ten differences?

Magical Music

These unicorn friends have formed a band, The Rainbow Rockers, and they hope to be famous one day!

Can you spot ten differences between the two
jam sessions?

Fruit Picking

These berries are ripe for the picking. Can you find six differences between the two rows of bushes?

Beautiful Blankets

Each unicorn keeps their own blanket in a particular place. Can you spot which two are out of position, by comparing the top picture to the bottom picture?

Mermaid Kingdom

King Poseidon is hosting a feast for all the merpeople!

Can you see ten differences between these two scenes?

Outer Space

Moonbeam is the first unicorn in space!

What wonders can she see on her space mission?
Find ten differences between the two starry scenes.

PICNIC IN THE PARK

Dragonfly and Roseleaf are enjoying a yummy picnic.
Can you spot six differences between the two pictures of them?

Pixie Parade

It's time for the annual pixie parade!
Can you find the pixie that looks a bit different?

Royal Wedding

Today is the day the fairy prince marries his fairy princess!

Everyone is so happy, and there's so much going on in the palace. Can you spot ten differences in the second picture?

Sunset Sky

These unicorns are watching the sun set over the ocean.
Can you find six differences between the two scenes?

Answers

3 Best Friends Forever

4-5 Rainbow Magic

6 Cupcake Count

7 Beautiful Butterflies

8-9 Kitten Kisses

10-11 Reindeer Replacements

12 Little Ones

13 Fancy Dress

14-15 Sparkling Sea

16-17 Dream Wings

18 Quickstep

19 Winter Wonderland

20-21 Falling Leaves

22-23 Splish Splash

24 Beach Bag

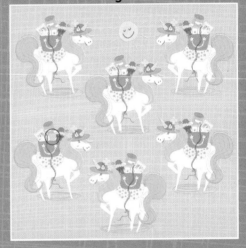

25 Love is in The Air

26-27 Brothers and Sisters

28-29 Sleepover Snuggles

30 Time to Shine

31 Prize Giving

32-33 Salon Style

34-35 Fairy Ring

36 Cloud Spotting

37 Flower Arranging

38-39 Princess Palace

40-41 Whiz, Pop, Bang!

42 Lucky Cakes

43 Flower Crown

44-45 Round and Round

46-47 Birthday Party

49 Puppy Pairs

50-51 Shopping Trip

48 Open Water

52-53 End of the Rainbow

54 Fairy Dust

55 Royal Jewels

56-57 Ice Skating

58-59 Ballet School

60 Kitten Tangle

61 Perfect Patterns

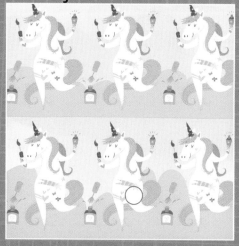

62-63 Christmas Carols

64-65 Sweet Dreams

66 Butterflies and Bees

67 Yummy Ice Creams

68-69 Fairground Fun

94

70-71 Coral Reef

72 Ski Slope

73 Uni-yoga

74-75 Gingerbread House

76-77 Magical Music

78 Fruit Picking

79 Beautiful Blankets

80-81 Mermaid Kingdom

82-83 Outer Space

84 Picnic In The Park

85 Pixie Parade

86-87 Royal Wedding

88 Sunset Sky